At School

by Lindsay Devick

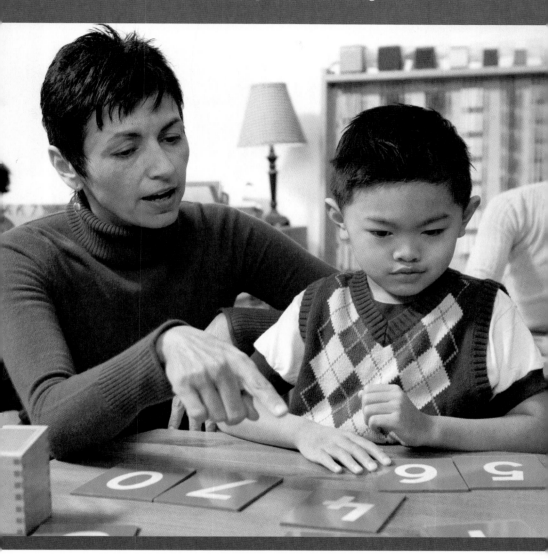

PEARSON

Glenview, Illinois • Boston, Massachusetts
Chandler, Arizona • Upper Saddle River, New Jersey

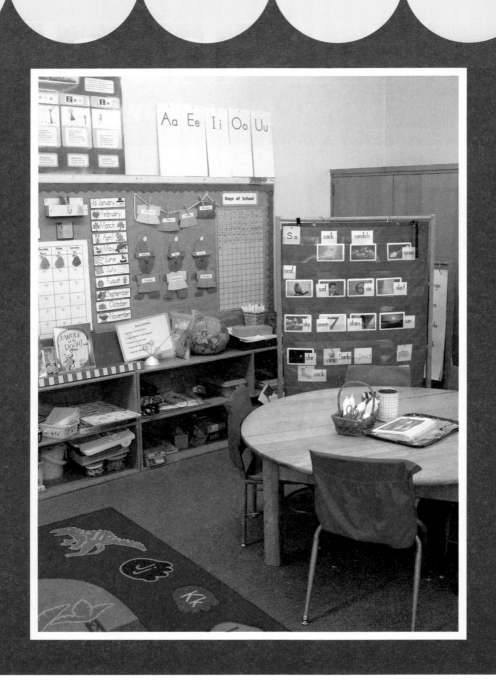

Time for school!

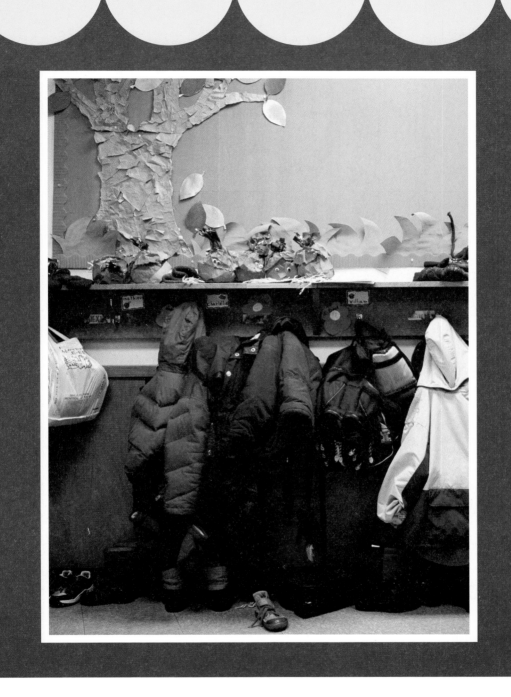

Coats go here.

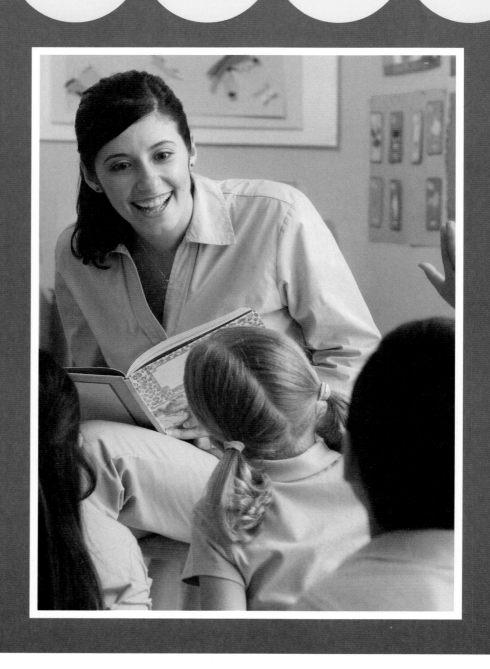

We read.

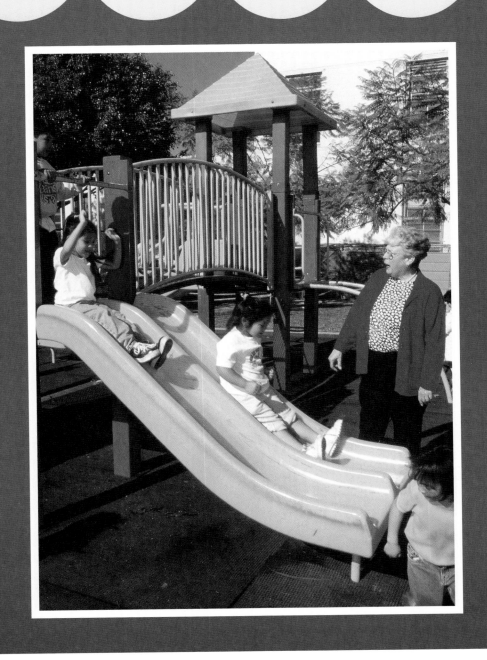

We play.

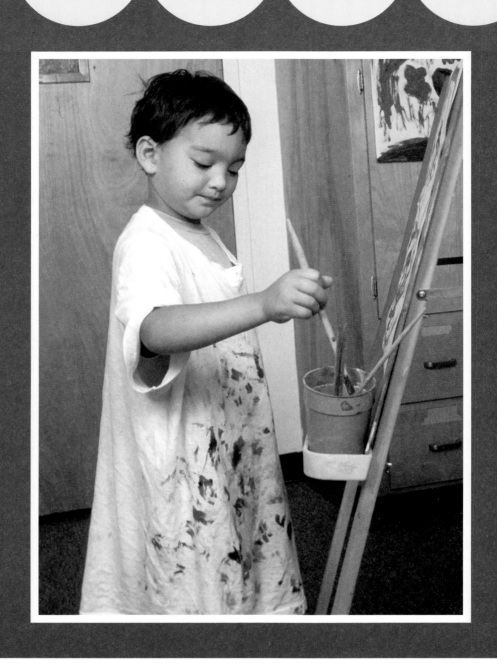

We paint.

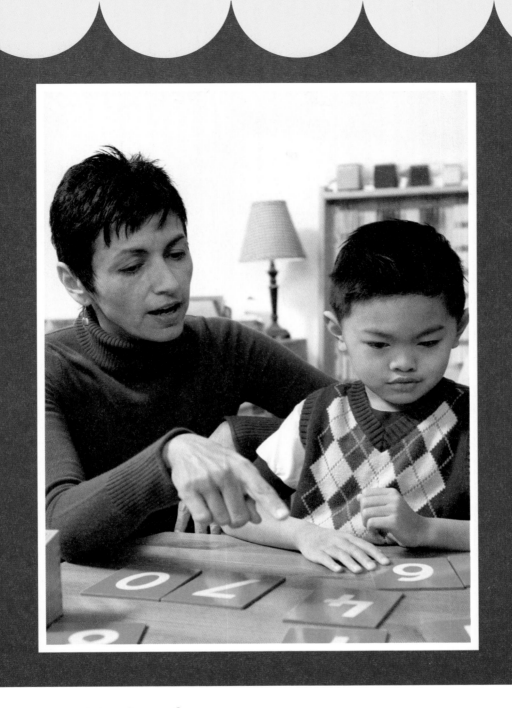

Math is fun.

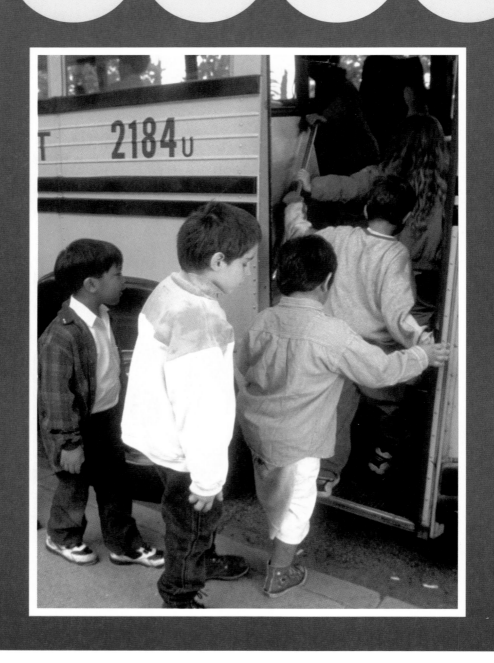

We go home.